This is a fictionalised biography describing some
of the key moments (so far!) in the career of
Robert Lewandowski.

Some of the events described in this book are
based upon the author's imagination and are
probably not entirely accurate representations
of what actually happened.

Tales from the Pitch
Robert Lewandowski
by Harry Coninx

Published in the United State of America and Canada
by Leapfrog Press
www.leapfrogpress.com

Distributed in the United States by
Consortium Book Sales and Distribution
St Paul, Minnesota 55114
www.cbsd.com

First Published in the United Kingdom by Raven Books
An imprint of Ransom Publishing Ltd.
Unit 7, Brocklands Farm, West Meon, Hampshire GU32 1JN, UK
www.ransom.co.uk

ISBN 978-1-948585-82-8
Also available as an eBook
First published in the United States 2023

TALES FROM THE PITCH

ROBERT LEWANDOWSKI

HARRY CONINX

Leapfrog Press
New York and London

For Daisy, who made these books what they are
(without even really understanding the basics of football)

CONTENTS

I

A THIRD DOUBLE

May 2019, Olympic Stadium, Berlin, Germany
Bayern Munich v RB Leipzig

A deafening roar filled Berlin's Olympic Stadium as the announcer read out the next name in the Bayern line-up.

"Number nine, ROBERT LEWANDOWSKIIIII!"

Robert sat in the dressing room, listened to the crowd screaming his name and smiled.

This was the DFB-Pokal Cup Final – the German

equivalent of the FA Cup – and Robert's opportunity to secure his third league and cup double. Yet he felt completely at ease.

"So if we get this, you could say you'll have done a hat-trick of doubles," Kingsley Coman mused, pulling up his socks.

Robert chuckled at the young French star, who he was about to play alongside in Bayern's attack.

They were also joined by winger Serge Gnabry, and Robert cast a glance over to where the kid was sitting, a little way away from the rest of the team. It was Serge's first final and he'd been quiet all day.

"You nervous, Serge?" Robert asked, approaching the young winger.

"A little bit," Serge said, as he fumbled with his boot laces.

"Don't be," Robert replied with a shrug. The advice was so weak and uninspiring that Serge couldn't help but laugh as he looked up at his team-mate.

"That's easy for you to say. You're Robert Lewandowski! You've probably scored the winning goal in every final you've played in!"

It always amused Robert that people seemed to think that he'd only ever been a superstar.

"Let's just go out there and have a good time," he said with a reassuring smile, before preparing himself mentally for the game at hand.

Bayern were taking on RB Leipzig, a team with plenty of top German players, who had pushed Bayern all the way in the Bundesliga. But Robert wasn't fazed.

Manuel Neuer got to his feet and made his way to the door. "We've won the league, lads. Now let's go out there and win this cup!"

Robert tilted his head from side to side, stretching his neck, then followed his captain. He was absolutely determined to return to the dressing room wearing a medal.

In what felt like no time the match had started and Bayern were on the move.

Half an hour in, and David Alaba had managed to get down the line and was about to cross the ball into the box.

Robert found himself a pocket of space, waited for the ball, then coolly flicked it towards the net with his head.

GOAL!

It was 1-0! Robert wheeled away towards the fans as they began chanting his name again, and looked over his shoulder to grin at his team-mates who were sprinting after him. He'd scored in countless finals, but it never made these moments any less special.

"What did I tell you?" Serge shouted in his ear, when he finally caught up with him, "You're Robert Lewandowski!"

The game was quickly back under way and Robert looked on as Bayern relied on their experienced keeper Manuel to make a number of top saves, keeping their narrow lead.

Robert knew they needed a second goal if they wanted to kill the game off.

Then, as if he'd read Robert's mind, Kingsley picked the ball up in the box and fired it into the top corner.

GOAL!

Robert punched the air, thrilled for the young winger.

He was sure that two goals would be enough to seal the win, but he was starting to get that familiar feeling – the feeling that he had another goal in him.

With a few minutes of the game remaining, the ball was pumped long and Robert saw his opportunity. He sprinted after it, shrugging off the Leipzig defender and bursting his way through, one-on-one.

He'd been in this situation a thousand times before, and he knew the range of techniques he had at his disposal. The keeper slid across the floor, so Robert opted just to dink the ball over him.

GOAL!

It was Robert's 40th goal of the season. He sprinted back towards the mass of cheering fans, this time leaping powerfully over the barrier to be closer to their delirious celebrations.

The whistle went, confirming that Bayern had won the game 3-0. They'd done the double – and Robert had acquired his hat-trick of doubles.

Back on the pitch the celebrations were hectic. Robert wasn't always sure who was hugging and congratulating him, but then he heard a voice he knew.

"Lewy!"

He turned to see Arjen Robben making his way towards him. This final was the veteran winger's last game for Bayern, and he came over and hugged Robert.

"You've got it – you've got the record for most goals scored in cup finals!" cried Arjen.

Robert threw back his head and looked up to the sky, as he sometimes did in moments like this. There were no words for what he was feeling; he just knew he never wanted it to stop.

By the time the medal and trophy ceremony had started, Robert's face was creased into a permanent smile.

He watched Manuel hold the German cup high in the air as the seemingly endless sea of Bayern fans waved their flags and cheered.

He knew that most people would call this moment the summit of his career. He was a record-breaking striker, at the centre of one of the best clubs in the world, and he'd won a multitude of trophies …

But Robert wasn't 'most people'. As he saw it, he still

hadn't reached the top, and he had big plans for what was next for 'Robert Lewandowski'.

2
MRS LEWANDOWSKA

May 1998, Robert's primary school, Leszno, Poland

Robert stood there, impatiently kicking at the ground out of boredom.

As always, he'd been the first to get changed into his sports kit, and now he was stuck waiting outside the gym for the rest of the class to get ready.

He sighed and decided to do some lunges to keep warm. He'd really tried to get ready slowly, like most of the kids, but he didn't want to waste a single second of PE. It was his all-time favourite lesson, and today they were focusing on his all-time favourite sport – football.

But for Robert, there was one massive downside to PE. His mum was the PE teacher.

At first it had been the most embarrassing thing in the world. Robert had been sure that she told him off more than any of the other kids, just to prove that she wasn't being soft on him, and it had often ended up in big arguments at home in the evening.

"I could see you weren't listening, Robert," his mum Iwona had shouted, as he'd stormed up the stairs after the first time she'd taught him. "You looked like you were in a complete daydream," she'd added, more amused than mad.

"I was," Robert had fired back, "I was imagining myself playing football for Poland!" And with that he'd slammed his bedroom door shut.

Robert's dad, Krzysztof, who'd been listening downstairs had chuckled at his son. He'd been exactly the same at that age.

But over time Robert had got more used to having

his mum teaching him. Sometimes he was even happy about it, even if he hated having to call her 'Mrs Lewandowska'.

She was actually really good at sport – she played professional volleyball – and he knew that her knowledge and experience could help him get to a similar level in football.

Robert kept that in mind as he watched her hurry the final stragglers out of the changing rooms and then gesture for the group to make their way to the school's sports field.

If he could stay in her good books today, he would be far more likely to get useful tips out of her.

Once the class had arrived at the field, he maintained a look of polite interest, to avoid any misunderstanding about him 'not listening' or 'daydreaming'.

His mum introduced the lesson and then gave everyone the option of either running drills or shooting practice.

It was a no-brainer for Robert and he was soon firing shots into an old, battered goal. Aleksander, his friend who was acting as the keeper, was getting increasingly frustrated at not being able to make any saves, but Robert just couldn't stop scoring. Top right, bottom left, smashed down the middle – he could do them all. He was smiling from ear to ear.

Robert had always been happiest with a ball at his feet. Between his mum's volleyball career and his dad being a Polish judo champion, he'd always been encouraged to have a go at lots of different sports. But Robert always said that football had chosen him.

His dad, who also played football for a local team, had been particularly thrilled.

"You'll be a superstar one day, son," he'd say during the two-hour drive each weekend to get nine-year-old Robert to his training with youth academy MKS Varsovia Warsaw.

The pair always used the time in the car to talk about the top Polish league, the Ekstraklasa, and Robert's promising future with it.

"That's exactly why I called you Robert," his dad exclaimed with a laugh, "It's a footballer's name! And a name that will be easy for all your fans around the world to chant!"

The sound of massed fans chanting his name was exactly what Robert was imagining as he pumped another shot past Aleksander into the back of the net.

"Make sure you practise with your left foot as well, Robert," he heard his mum say behind him. He immediately fired one into the goal with his left foot, and turned to her with a grin.

"And maybe it's Aleksander's turn to shoot now," she added.

It was the most annoying thing she could have said, and Robert couldn't avoid pulling a face at her, before reluctantly swapping places with his friend.

He'd hear about that at home, no doubt.

3
CLUB-LESS

April 2006, Legia Warsaw training ground, Warsaw

As Robert stood on the sideline and watched his Legia Warsaw II team-mates going through their training, he accidentally made eye contact with his manager.

Robert had heard the rumours going around that he was at risk of being dropped by Legia, so he quickly gave the manager a big (fake) smile. He didn't want to give anybody a reason to make the rumours a reality.

Robert had worked hard chasing his dream career in the Ekstraklasa, going from his first club, the academy MKS Varsovia Warsaw, to Delta Warsaw, and then to Legia Warsaw, one of the biggest clubs in Poland.

He wasn't going to let all that effort go to waste – especially as he hadn't even got out of the reserve team yet.

Out on the pitch, the ball bounced over a defender and rolled past a striker. Robert could only imagine how he would have brought it down with one touch and then slammed it neatly into the bottom corner of the net.

He sighed deeply. This injury he'd been nursing for the last few months just couldn't have come at a worse time. He needed to be playing now more than ever, to secure his place at the club.

Still, to show willing, he made sure he attended training almost every day. At least then he could listen to the coaching talks, so it wouldn't seem as if he'd missed out on too much when he finally got back on the pitch.

He'd also realised that you could learn a lot just by watching the training sessions. There were things you could see from a distance that you couldn't see when you were on the pitch, playing in the heat of the moment. For example, he began to notice all the spaces in the box that the strikers weren't using.

"Get in those spaces and you'll score," he muttered to himself.

The practice game soon drew to a close and the players started making their way back to the dressing room.

Robert was just about to follow his friends when he heard his manager calling his name. He turned and made his way over to him as quickly as possible. The manager didn't look happy.

"Listen, Robert, this isn't something I like having to do, but I can't watch you coming to training any more," his manager said, before pausing for what felt like hours. "The club has come to a decision about your future. We're concerned you won't cut it at a higher level, so we've decided that we're going to have to let you go."

Robert felt as if he'd been punched in the stomach. He opened his mouth, but shut it straight away. He thought he might burst into tears if he spoke, so he just nodded slowly.

"I'm sorry, son. It's always a shame when these things don't work out. We'll get the paperwork sent through to your agent." He patted Robert on the shoulder, before leaving him alone on the pitch.

Robert just stood there, watching his breath in the cold spring air, as his mind went into overdrive.

By the time each of his parents had turned sixteen they'd already been well on the way to the highest levels of their respective sports. Yet here *he* was, seventeen, club-less, and with no other offers on the table.

Football was all he'd ever wanted to do. It couldn't be over already.

Out of the corner of his eye, Robert could see a ball that had been left on the pitch after training, and he found himself walking over to it. He nudged it with his foot. The thought that hurt the most was how disappointed his dad would have been.

Over the next few days it broke his mum Iwona's heart to watch her son drift around the house. It had almost been a year now since Krzysztof had died, and she knew that losing his place in his dad's favourite team would crush her son.

She'd also known that she had to do something to help, but as she peered around the open door and saw Robert sitting on the sofa, looking into space, she wasn't sure how well her news was going to be received.

"Listen, Robert, I've been in contact with the coach at Znicz Pruszków," Iwona said gently, sitting next down next to him. "They're hoping to be promoted to the second division this year and they'd love to have you on their team."

"That would be a huge step down," Robert mumbled sadly. He was at an age when he should be making progress in his career, not going backwards. All the work he and his dad had put in, the countless hours driving to and from practice – all of it had been wasted.

"Don't think of it as a step down, Rob," his mum replied brightly. "Think of it as a way to get your foot back on the ladder. Once you're back on the ladder – *then* you can put your effort into climbing your way to the top."

There was a long silence, which Iwona felt the need to fill. "And, more important, you'll be able to get back to doing what you love."

The silence continued as Iwona tried to work out what her son was thinking.

"Sign for Znicz Pruszków," she urged one last time.

Robert suddenly turned to look at her, and she could see a different glint in his eyes.

"Yes, Mrs Lewandowska," he said, with a small but cheeky smile. Iwona's heart lifted at the sight and she gave him a tight hug.

Robert knew his mum was right. It didn't matter where he was, as long as he was training, playing and improving.

Once she'd left him alone in the room, he got to his feet and walked over to the window. The sky outside was a striking blue, and he thought of his dad looking down on him.

The only thing that would have really disappointed his dad would be if Robert gave up on the dreams they'd always shared.

He wasn't going to do that. Instead, Robert silently

promised himself that he was going to prove everyone wrong.

He was going to make it to the very top of football, whatever it took.

4
ON THE LADDER

July 2007, Stadion Miejski, Lowicz, Poland
Znicz Pruszków v Pelikan Lowicz

When Robert joined Znicz Pruszków he wasn't the quickest, the strongest or the most skilful player in the team.

But the coaches had never seen anyone quite so determined to improve. Together with his natural ruthlessness in the box, he seemed to have everything they were looking for in a young striker, and they had quickly started nurturing him as a potential lethal striker for the team.

"You're a big lad," one of the coaches had said. "Get yourself between the ball and the defender – completely shield it."

"And as soon as you get even a glimpse of goal, pull the trigger," another coach had advised. "If you don't score, the keeper might parry it straight to one of our players."

Robert had absorbed everything they'd told him and he'd developed at a fantastic rate in his first season.

Now, as he bounded out on to the pitch for the first game of his second season with the club, Robert felt a surge of pride. He'd scored 16 goals last season – goals which had made this dream promotion to the second division a reality for Znicz.

"If you get a chance, cross it to Robbie!" their coach was mouthing from the sideline with exaggerated gestures. The whole team exchanged smiles. When was that ever *not* the game plan?

The match started slowly and Robert stayed up front, close to the box. He didn't get much of the ball and his strike partner, Bartosz Wiśniewski, was actually the first to score a goal.

"This isn't the third division anymore," Bartosz whispered, as Robert pulled him over for a celebratory hug. "We need a second goal if we're going to kill the game."

Robert nodded. Bartosz was right.

Robert saw his chance to provide that second goal when the ball was back at their end. As he'd learnt by watching Legia's training when he'd been injured, there was always a pocket of space in the box to exploit, and now he saw it and made his way into it.

A whipped cross from the left suddenly sailed towards him and he slashed at the ball.

GOAL!

The Znicz fans jumped to their feet as his team-mates sprinted over to him. It was 2-0!

"This is too easy for you, man," one of them gabbled in his ear.

"How do you keep doing it?" another shouted. "You only get about five touches, but you seem to score in every game!"

Robert didn't have an answer, so he just enjoyed the moment and laughed at the praise.

He had officially started this new season exactly as he meant to go on, and he hoped that every scout in the world was watching.

Now he was firmly on the ladder – all he had to do was climb it.

5

THE NEXT STEP

June 2008, Cezary Kucharski's office, Warsaw, Poland

As Robert looked across the table at his agent, Cezary Kucharski, he felt a deep fondness for the man.

Before becoming a football agent, Cezary had actually played the game – as a striker. He'd been good enough to play for Poland, too.

But today Cezary was especially favoured. He'd called Robert in to give him some good news.

"Sporting Gijón in Spain are interested in you, Rob. What do you think?"

Robert's eyes widened at the fact that clubs from abroad were considering him for their team. It shouldn't have been much of a surprise, though.

The last season had raced by and he'd finished as the top scorer in the second division, with 21 goals. Znicz Pruszków had only narrowly missed out on another promotion, and all eyes were on the boy who was dragging them up through the Polish divisions.

It was all a far cry from when he'd first joined the club as a last resort, knowing that nobody else had wanted him.

Robert turned his attention back to the conversation.

"I'm not really sure about leaving Poland, Cezary. I mean, this is my home."

"OK, I hear you," Cezary said with a nod. Sporting Gijón had been Cezary's former club, and it would have been a nice touch if Robert had gone for them. He knew that the Spanish first division would be a huge opportunity for a player like Robert, who was in a hurry to be the best.

"So, back to the Polish offers. There's Lech Poznań. They – "

"Lech Poznań?" Robert interrupted. They were one of the biggest teams in Poland.

"You like them, huh?" Cezary asked.

Robert nodded eagerly. His thoughts went straight back to that conversation with his mum.

He was on the ladder, taking it step by step, and this was going to be the next step.

"I'll call them," said Cezary with a smile.

6
BY ROBERT'S HEEL

August 2008, Stadion Miejski, Poznań, Poland
Lech Poznań v GKS Bełchatów

Robert sat on the bench as the game against GKS
Bełchatów got underway. He knew that his debut for
Lech Poznań had to be something special; he wanted to
send a message to the rest of Poland – and this was his
chance.

Technically, he'd already played for the club in a
UEFA Cup qualifying round. That had been against

a team from Azerbaijan, and Robert had come on at half-time.

Within 20 minutes he'd changed that game when a ball rebounded to him on the edge of the box. The advice from his old coaches had now become instinctive and he'd tried a shot as soon as it came to him.

The ball had slammed into the back of the net and his new team-mates had showered him with praise.

Robert had been completely thrilled, but even then a little part of him knew that, to make his mark, he needed to do the same in his league debut against a more challenging side.

Now that day was here.

He tried to relax and watch the game in his new home stadium, but as the minutes passed he became more anxious, totally aware of how tricky it can be to make an impact when you're a late sub.

He pushed these worries to the back of his mind. He wasn't going to let anything stop him, even if they brought him on in the 89th minute.

At last, late in the second half, Robert's moment came and he made his way on to the pitch.

His new team-mates smiled at him encouragingly. After his performance in their last match, they were confident Robert wouldn't disappoint – and they were right.

Just four minutes later, he was running straight down the middle, well ahead of the defenders.

He could see the goal and the ball coming in to him, but he knew he was in a bit of an awkward position to just turn and kick it.

Robert felt his mind relax as he allowed his instincts to take over. He let the ball run through his legs, before catching it with his heel and flicking it towards the net, mid-sprint.

GOAL!

"The new kid's a legend already!" one of his team-mates shouted, as they huddled around him.

The Lech fans were going wild in the stands and Robert was quick to give them a little wave, before getting stuck back into the game.

He was already hungry for the next time he could bring them to their feet.

7

FOR POLAND

September 2008, Lech Poznań training ground,
Poznań, Poland

"Yes, I know who you are," Robert spluttered down the phone.

Leo Beenhakker was actually the first person Robert had thought of when he'd been called into his manager's office to 'take a call'. But he'd immediately dismissed the thought.

Robert couldn't be the only player who, on being told

there was a phone call for him, immediately thought it might be from the manager of his national team. After all, that was the one call every footballer in the world dreamt of getting.

"Good, then you've probably guessed why I'm ringing. I want you in my squad for the next run of fixtures," Leo said.

Robert put his hand over his mouth to stifle his gasp. He was suddenly overcome with emotion by how far he'd come. From being told he wouldn't 'cut it' at a higher level, he'd clawed his way up to become the main striker for a team in the Ekstraklasa, and now, aged just twenty, he'd be joining the senior national team.

"I'd love to," he finally managed to say, hoping Leo wouldn't mistake the wobble in his voice for a lack of confidence.

He'd already proved he could handle the pressure of debuts twice over with Lech, and this debut would be no different. He was already planning nothing less than a spectacular goal for his country.

Sitting on the bench in San Marino's national stadium, Robert couldn't stop looking down at the big red number 13 on his chest. He already adored his white Poland shirt and would constantly try to catch his reflection in shiny surfaces whenever he pulled it on.

His team-mate Jakub Błaszczykowski had laughed when he'd caught him doing it in the dressing rooms.

"I'm not sure playing for Poland suits you, Rob!" he'd teased.

Robert's other team-mate, Łukasz Piszczek, had quickly got involved in the banter. "Look! Now he's blushing – that extra bit of red looks a lot better!"

Robert had laughed with his new friends and jokingly gestured for them to leave him alone. The atmosphere had been light back then, but now he was looking out at the small stadium he could feel some nerves bubbling in the pit of his stomach.

His opportunity to guarantee himself a future place in the Poland side had arrived, although he'd only get it if he was brought on. He'd had to watch the whole of the last game from the bench, and today could easily go the same way.

But, with Poland leading San Marino 1-0, Leo eventually gestured for him to come over.

Robert walked over, dazzled by the opportunity. This was the stuff of his childhood imagination – the stuff of his endless chats with his dad in the car as he'd been driven to and from training.

"Go on, kid," Leo said as he slapped Robert on the back. "Go and see if you can grab yourself a goal!"

Robert nodded and steadily jogged out on to the pitch. He could see Jakub giving him a little round of applause and Łukasz giving him a big 'thumbs up'.

He already loved being a part of this team, and wanted to score for his team-mates as much as for himself.

The game got back underway and it didn't take Robert long to notice that the San Marino pitch was exactly like the ones he'd been playing on in the lower divisions not too long ago. He was completely at home with this – unlike a lot of his team-mates, who had only played for bigger clubs and were sometimes thrown by pitches that weren't absolutely top quality.

He'd only been on for eight minutes when the ball

bobbled into the box and a shot swung it towards goal. The ball clipped the post and Robert was the first to react as it bounced back into play. He poked it straight into the back of the net.

He hadn't really thought about what he was doing – once again it was all instinctive – but now, as his team-mates rushed over to him, the adrenalin hit.

"My bad! Playing for Poland clearly does suit you!" Jakub yelled as he pulled Robert in for a hug. Łukasz babbled on about how Robert had to be one of the youngest players ever to score on their debut.

It was only when his friends started moving away for the game to continue that Robert looked up the sky to share a brief moment with his dad. Robert wanted that goal, his first for Poland, to be for him.

The rest of the match went by in a flash and Poland ran out 2-0 winners. Only after the match did somebody confirm that Łukasz had *almost* been right. Robert was the *second* youngest player ever to score on their Poland debut.

It was a great result all round. Leo was proud, the team were proud, and Robert knew that his mum, watching back home on the TV, would be proud. She could officially add his name to the list of family members who'd represented Poland in their sport.

That was a thought that filled Robert with optimism as he bounded off the pitch. He was very aware that his country had never been one of the great footballing nations, but he wanted to change that.

If he was climbing a ladder to greatness, he saw no reason why he couldn't take his national team with him.

8
ON TOP

May 2010, Stadion Miejski, Poznań, Poland
Lech Poznań v Zagłębie Lubin

The previous season, Robert's first in top-flight Polish football, had ended with silverware when Lech Poznań found their way into the Polish Cup Final, winning 1-0.

But it hadn't been because of Robert.

He'd had a fantastic season, but in that final Robert had slashed at a few chances and had wasted crucial opportunities to put his side ahead.

He wasn't used to missing, and had been very concerned to see that his usually lethal finishing form had abandoned him.

"I don't know what's happening to me," he moaned to his team-mate Hernán Rengifo in training, as he put another shot straight down the keeper's throat.

"That's the pressure of professional football for you, buddy. Sometimes your mind goes blank and everything goes out of the window," Hernán replied. He tapped the side of his head as he continued. "You may know how to control the ball, but you've got to learn to control yourself."

Fortunately, Hernán's experience had shone through in that cup final and he'd been able to slip the ball to Sławomir Peszko, who'd fired it past the keeper.

Robert had naturally celebrated the 1-0 win and his first major trophy with the team, but he hadn't been able to shake his frustration at how he'd handled the pressure of a final.

Now, after another year with the club, he was ready to

show everyone how far he'd come. Today was the final game of the season, against Zagłębie Lubin, and there was a league title at stake.

"We all know what we need to do out there, boys!" the gaffer, Jacek Zieliński, said to them as they prepared for the game.

Then he held up three fingers. It was the three points they needed from this match to snatch the title from current champions Wisła Kraków.

The team were up for it. They'd already won the Polish Super Cup back in July and everyone was eager to add a second trophy to their season's haul.

Robert was no exception, and he strode determinedly out onto the pitch. The stadium filled with smoke as thousands of Lech fans released flares, and the sight only inspired Robert more.

He'd scored four goals in his last three games and was not going to let the stress of another crucial game affect his performance.

The opposition, however, were definitely affected by the occasion, and within half an hour an own goal from one of the Zagłębie defenders gave Lech the lead.

Robert could practically feel the weight of the third major trophy of his career in his hands, but he still wanted to do what he'd failed to do last year – score.

Suddenly he saw the ball go out to the wing and fly into the box. A defender tried to boot it clear, but miskicked it and the ball flew into the air.

It was a mistake that Robert pounced on. As had so often happened on previous occasions, he relaxed and let instinct take over. All that mattered was getting the ball past the keeper. He put his foot through it and watched as it rippled the back of the net.

GOAL!

The Lech fans erupted, waving flags and lighting more flares.

Robert cheered with them as the other players rushed over to him. As they celebrated, he made sure to catch Hernán's eye as he tapped the side of his head. Hernán instantly remembered their conversation and laughed.

The match ended with Lech securing the three points they needed, and for the first time in 17 years they were declared champions of Poland.

Robert soaked up the incredible atmosphere and

looked around triumphantly. He'd won a Polish Cup, the Polish Super Cup and an Ekstraklasa title with this team. It was the complete set, and his heart swelled with pride, knowing that he was now at the very top of Polish football.

The thought, however, brought a certain sadness as well. If he was at the top, he knew he'd probably gone as far as he could with Lech.

Now he needed a bigger dream.

9
ON THE MOVE

July 2010, Cezary's office, Warsaw, Poland

Sitting in Cezary's office, Robert had a strong sense of déjà vu. Not for the first time, he was listening to Cezary running through the names of all the teams who were interested in signing him.

But now there was one big difference. Now Robert had a strong scoring record, as well as some trophies under his belt. It was a thought that made him very happy – and it meant that he could be a lot more choosy when it came to negotiating with clubs.

Robert hadn't actually planned on a meeting with Cezary today. The pair had both thought that he was going to join Blackburn Rovers in England.

Robert had been about to fly over to discuss the details of his move, when an Icelandic volcano had erupted and spewed ash out all over Europe. All flights had been cancelled and Robert couldn't make it to the meeting.

The world of football is a very impatient one, and Blackburn gave up on the idea of buying him, saying only that it was a shame it didn't work out.

Robert had heard these kinds of words before, but this time he was able to brush them off. He knew there would be plenty more options available to him, and anyway he hadn't been too sure about Blackburn in the first place.

His confidence wasn't misplaced, and he sipped at some water while Cezary reeled off the names of all the other clubs that had expressed interested in him.

He was instantly struck by one name: Borussia Dortmund, in Germany.

"Their manager, Jürgen Klopp, says they're going to try and win the league next year," Cezary shrugged.

"What? They're going to beat Bayern Munich?" Robert asked, quite surprised.

"Well, *they* think they will," Cezary replied. "So, should I tell them 'no'?"

"No, no," Robert said. Something deep inside him told him he couldn't say 'no' to this one. But there was another voice inside his head, the same voice that had told him to say no to Sporting Gijón and he had been quietly thankful that the move to Blackburn hadn't come off.

Robert realised that, deep down, he was not keen to leave Poland. He was only 21 years old, and it was scary to think that the ladder he was climbing led away from his family, his friends and everything he'd ever known.

But he also couldn't ignore the fact that this was something he needed to do for his career. The Bundesliga was one of the biggest leagues in the world and would develop his football in ways that playing in Poland never could.

He thought back to the promise he'd made himself

all those years ago, the promise to make it to the top, whatever it took.

He took a deep breath.

"I want to do it. Tell them, 'Yes'."

Robert had spent the last two weeks trying to convince himself he'd made the right choice, but he was finding life in Dortmund tough.

He knew that geographically he wasn't far from Poland, but some days it felt as if his home was a million miles away – and then his homesickness would hang heavily over him.

The biggest issue was the fact he barely knew any German, and he could kick himself for not having paid closer attention to his language lessons in school.

German lessons had always come right before PE and he'd spent all his time counting down the minutes before he'd be free to race to the changing rooms.

Now, here he was, living in Germany, and the only word he knew in German was 'Danke'.

The club had very good translators and most of the

players and coaches spoke English, but none of that helped with how isolating it felt to hear conversations bubbling around him and have no idea what people were talking about. Or to look at a sign or a menu and always have to ask what it said.

Luckily, Robert did have one saving grace. Or, more accurately, two: Łukasz and Jakub. The two friends he'd made on international duty were both also playing at Dortmund, and the three Poles were quickly inseparable.

They warmed up together, ate together and even hung out together in the evenings. They really were a little taste of home for Robert, and if it wasn't for them he wasn't sure he would still be in Germany.

The trio were just enjoying a short break at a club training session, with Robert making the others laugh with tales of his short-lived volleyball career (as an eight-year-old!), when their joking was cut short.

Robert's name was being called from across the pitch – and he didn't have to turn around to know it was Jürgen Klopp. Robert had seen him stalking the training ground earlier in the morning and he wondered if this would be his first chance to speak with his new manager.

He obediently jogged straight over to where Jürgen was standing.

"How are you finding things in Germany?" Jürgen asked.

"Good," Robert lied. Jürgen met his eye and Robert felt as if he could see right through him. "It's nice to have the lads here," he added, more honestly, gesturing to Jakub and Łukasz, "And I'm excited to get going in the Bundesliga."

"Ah, I'm sure you've heard I want to go for the title this year – I really believe we can do it," Jürgen said.

Robert nodded and felt invigorated. This was the kind of ambition that had persuaded him to join Dortmund in the first place. Like him, Jürgen was somebody used to aiming high.

"We play a very specific style of football here," Jürgen continued. "It's very high energy, lots of running, lots of expression. Football is about having fun, right?" he said with a wide smile.

Robert nodded again. Jürgen's enthusiasm was simply

infectious, and it was exactly what Robert needed. He could feel his thoughts of home receding and football once again taking centre-stage.

There and then, he resolved to make this move to Germany work.

He saw that Jürgen had already started to walk away, so he quickly called after him.

"Hey boss, do you think I could have a couple more German lessons a week?"

Jürgen turned with a slightly puzzled but cheerful expression.

"Ja, natürlich," he replied.

10
DERBY DRAMA

September 2010, Veltins Arena, Gelsenkirchen, Germany
Schalke v Borussia Dortmund

Robert worked hard to adapt to life in Germany, and he was slowly adapting to German football under Jürgen. At times it felt as if the football was the hardest to get used to.

Back in Poland he'd been a big fish in a small pond, but here it was painfully clear he was a tiny fish in a huge ocean of Bundesliga talent.

He still cringed when he remembered his debut for Dortmund, against Bayern Leverkusen.

He'd looked on from the bench as Leverkusen had put two past Dortmund in a matter of minutes, leaving the normally loud Dortmund crowd shell-shocked.

Then, 20 minutes into the second half, he'd been sent on for his debut, and on his very first touch he'd been clattered off the ball by Leverkusen defender Sami Hyypiä. He'd not even had the chance to look up and find a pass.

As the game went on he'd continued to struggle to make any sort of an impact. Every player had been quicker, stronger and technically better than any he'd ever faced before.

Lucas Barrios had felt so sorry for him that he'd actually jogged over and offered to swap places.

Compared to his incredible debuts for Lech and Poland, it had been a massive reality check and the thought that Germany wasn't the right place for him had come surging back as he'd trudged off the pitch.

But Robert had ignored it. He knew what he'd committed himself to – he'd just have to push himself even harder in training and try to get a goal for Dortmund in their next game.

At it turned out, their next game was a huge local derby, away to Schalke.

As was becoming normal, Robert started the game on the bench. He used the time to soak up the incredible atmosphere that only a derby could bring.

It was obvious that this game meant so much more to the fans and Robert found the crowd's passion inspiring.

He hadn't scored on his debut, but scoring in this derby would be a good alternative. And what's more, if he managed it, it would be in the presence of one of the best strikers of all time – Schalke's Raúl.

"Do you not get what a big deal this is? Being on the same pitch as Raúl?" Robert said to Jakub, who was sitting on the bench next to him. Jakub didn't hear him – his attention was on the game that was about to begin.

Shinji Kagawa quickly put Dortmund in the lead,

and the Japanese international doubled that lead in the second half.

Dortmund were in control of the game and Jürgen gradually started to bring on each of his subs in turn.

"You up for this?" he asked Robert, when his chance came.

"Of course," Robert said determinedly. "Or should I say, 'Ja, natürlich'?" His German was getting better by the day and he was ready to show how much his hard work in training had been paying off as well.

The pair exchanged a quick knowing smile and then Robert was out on the pitch. Being a late sub had never stopped him from scoring back in Poland – and he wasn't going to let it stop him now.

With about five minutes left to play, Dortmund won a corner. Robert shut everyone out, found himself the perfect space in the box and waited.

The ball came flying over and, harnessing all his frustration from the past two months, he launched himself off the floor. He rose high above the Schalke defence and looped a header into the top corner.

GOAL!

In that split-second when the ball crossed over the line, all the struggles Robert had been facing over the past two months melted away. Missing home, the exhausting training sessions, the language problems – they were all worth it just for this moment.

He sprinted towards the small section of Dortmund fans, not quite sure what he was doing and completely caught up in the moment.

He looked up to see them on their feet, thrilled at the way their team were humiliating their local rivals and at the same time surging to the top of the Bundesliga. Knowing he'd finally contributed to both of those outcomes was pure bliss.

By the end of the match Robert felt as if he was walking on air and he barely noticed whose hand he was shaking. Then, three words in a thick Spanish accent brought him back down to earth.

"Good goal, man."

Robert's eyes widened as he stared into Raúl's face. Hearing those words from the ex-Real Madrid striker confirmed it for him – Germany was exactly where he was meant to be.

He wasn't going anywhere.

II

CAN'T STOP SCORING

May 2012, Robert's hotel room, Berlin, Germany

Robert lay back on his hotel bed and tapped 'Call' on his phone.

He'd usually spend his time before a cup final mentally preparing himself, but today he was feeling incredibly relaxed so he thought he'd ring his mum instead.

This was his second season with Dortmund, and

since it had started he just hadn't stopped scoring. He didn't feel that today would be any different.

As he listened to the phone ringing, he thought back to the conversation he'd had with Jürgen last year, a conversation that seemed to have started this goal-scoring spree.

"I don't know if I'm cut out for the Bundesliga, boss," he'd sighed to his manager. "I just don't know if I'm going to get the goals I did in Poland."

Since scoring in the derby against Schalke, Robert had really struggled his way through the season, and it had looked as if he was going to end it with just eight measly goals to his name.

Jürgen had looked him up and down before speaking.

"How many of our players do you think were superstars when we signed them?" he'd asked.

"I don't know."

"Lucas had played for about five clubs in South America when we brought him in. Shinji had never played outside Japan. Half our players came through the academy."

Robert had been puzzled, not quite understanding Klopp's point.

"What I'm saying is, we don't buy superstars here at Dortmund. We *make* them. So don't worry if you're struggling – it's something we'll work on together."

And they had done. Jürgen had even given Robert one-on-one finishing training, where he'd win 50 euros off the manager if he scored 10 goals.

It had been the vote of confidence Robert needed. He'd even managed to finish his abysmal season with a goal in a title decider.

He could still remember chanting "CHAMPIONES! CHAMPIONES! OLE OLE OLE!" with the rest of his team – now officially the best in Germany – as if it were yesterday.

His thoughts were interrupted when his mum suddenly answered his call.

"Hello Robbie, so sorry, I'd left my phone upstairs and couldn't find it. How are you? How are Łukasz and Jakub? How are you feeling about today?" she rambled.

"That's OK, I'm OK, they're OK," he chuckled.

"*Good* actually. I'm starting to get a sixth sense for when I'm going to score." He was only half-joking.

"After all your goals, I'm not surprised!" she said. "You're on 27 this season, aren't you?"

"For the moment," Robert replied. He had high hopes for this afternoon's game. "My favourite is still the one I scored last month that won us the Bundesliga again," he told her.

"My son, a two-time Bundesliga champion!" his mum exclaimed. "You know how proud I am, don't you? Your dad would be proud too."

Robert beamed at the words, as his mum went on.

"It's almost as if you're being greedy with the goals now – just like when I used to teach your PE classes and catch you not giving your little friends a chance!"

"You're not suggesting I stop scoring?" Robert teased. Even though she'd retired from volleyball a long time ago, he knew that at heart she was still a fiercely competitive athlete.

"Absolutely not," his mum replied sharply, taking Robert's bait. "Don't you let Mr Klopp down today!"

"Do you know what's better than winning the league?" Jürgen asked everyone in the changing room later that day.

He paused dramatically before answering his own question. "Winning the league *and* the cup. And that's what I want us to have achieved by the end of today."

Robert loved the way Jürgen was never satisfied, constantly chasing the next thing that could be achieved. It always fired him up, and looking around the room he could see it was having the same effect on the rest of the team.

Nobody looked at all fazed by the fact that in this cup final they were about to meet their biggest rivals.

Bayern Munich.

This positive attitude was carried on to the pitch and, only a few minutes into the game, Robert found himself tussling with Jérôme Boateng on the edge of the box. He was well used to the pace and physicality of the German defenders now, and he managed to get the ball to Shinji Kagawa, who tucked it into the back of the net.

Bayern were soon back in it when Arjen Robben

converted a penalty, but Dortmund were then awarded a penalty – which Mats Hummels tucked away.

It was turning into an end-to-end game, and with half-time fast approaching, the ball fell to Robert. His first touch took him into the box, and his second saw the ball slip between Manuel Neuer's legs and nestle in the back of the net.

GOAL! 3-1 to Dortmund.

Dortmund kept up the pressure in the second half. Kevin Großkreutz fed Robert a quick ball and he slammed it as hard as he could. It whistled past Neuer, making it 4-1.

"What a strike!" Shinji shouted as he leaped on to Robert's shoulders.

The cheers of the Dortmund fans showed that they were thinking the same thing, and the noise only charged Robert up even more.

Franck Ribéry managed a goal to pull Bayern back into the game, but it was in vain. Robert was far too confident to let this slip now, and a hat-trick felt like an inevitability.

Suddenly a mistake from Neuer gave the ball to

Łukasz, who managed to cross it into the box. Robert came piling in and crashed a header into the empty net. He'd turned to begin celebrating the goal even before he'd seen the ball cross the line.

The game was won – and Dortmund had done the double.

"*That's* the Robert Lewandowski I signed!" Jürgen bellowed as Robert ran to join the rest of the players, who were jumping around in front of their fans.

Robert beamed at his manager's praise and quietly wished that his old team-mate Hernán Rengifo from Lech was here, so he could tap the side of his head at him again. He'd come a long way from his goal-less cup final in the Ekstraklasa.

"This is a new era in German football!" Łukasz roared next to him.

Robert knew his friend was talking to the fans more than to any of the players, but the words struck a chord with him. He'd helped Znicz get promoted, he'd helped Lech get to the top of Polish football and now, after a year of hard work, his 30 goals this season had helped Dortmund get to the top of German football.

The thought of some kind of 'Robert effect' filled him with excitement for the summer ahead. Poland was co-hosting the European Championships with Ukraine, and he was determined to help his national team to new heights.

It was something he'd wanted to do ever since he'd walked off the pitch in San Marino.

12
EUROS AT HOME

June 2012, Stadion Narodowy, Warsaw, Poland
Poland v Greece

"I'm not going to downplay it, lads. Today's game will probably be one of the most important games of your careers," new Poland manager Franciszek Smuda said firmly.

The nervous chatter in the changing room was cut dead and all the players turned to look at him.

"Most players are lucky to get to play for their country

at all, let alone at a major tournament – and especially a major tournament at home."

Franciszek paused and looked around the room. "So make sure you give it your all."

Before his manager had even finished speaking Robert had jumped to his feet.

Not only was he itching to get some goals for Poland, this Euros was his first international tournament and today was the first game of the entire competition.

It was an opportunity to announce himself on the world stage and he was more than ready, coming to it on the back of the best season of his career.

Out on the pitch, Robert took a moment to eye up the opposition. Greece had won the Euros back in 2004, against all the odds, and Robert saw them as an inspiration for Poland – proof that the underdog could still win a major tournament.

Robert knew that this time around Poland had to be in with a real chance. No doubt this was one of the strongest squads Poland had had in a long time.

Cheered on by the boisterous home crowd, Poland made a dominant start to the game and Jakub was soon pulling away down the right-hand side with the ball.

Robert had anticipated what was about to happen, so he'd moved away from the defenders and drifted towards their back post. It was the same combination that had worked for Dortmund over and over again.

Jakub whipped the ball into the box and Robert met it with his head.

GOAL!

Robert had just scored the first goal of the 2012 Euros – *and* in front of a home crowd!

He sprinted towards the thousands of screaming fans, not quite knowing how to channel his energy. He could feel himself half-running and half-jumping, so he decided to make one massive leap into the air. When he landed, there was a split second when he felt as if he and the crowd were the only ones there.

The moment ended as his team-mates piled on top of him, every single one of them babbling words of congratulations.

Their celebrations, however, were cut short when

Greece equalized, and from that point onwards Poland were lucky to stay in the game.

It pained Robert to watch their strong start go to waste, and at the final whistle the scores were still level.

Robert consoled himself with the knowledge that he had made something of this opportunity on the world stage. No one could take that once-in-a-lifetime goal away from him, and he stayed on the pitch as long as he could, soaking up the scene so he would remember this momentous occasion.

"What a moment, Robbie!" Jakub said, wrapping his arms around Robert and eventually dragging him towards the tunnel. "You must be losing count of all your goals by now. But I reckon you'll remember that one."

13

CHAMPIONS LEAGUE LADDER

August 2012, Dortmund training ground,
Dortmund, Germany

Robert returned to Dortmund after the summer break. He still found it hard coming to terms with the fact that his grand plans for Poland in the Euros hadn't played out the way he'd wanted. He knew there would be other chances for him to lead the team to victory, but crashing out at the group stages was still weighing heavily on him.

Combined with the loss of Shinji and Lucas from

the Dortmund squad and the fact that today was Dortmund's first training session since they'd lost to Bayern Munich in the German Super Cup, his morale was a little low.

Nevertheless he tried to stay positive as Jürgen gathered the team together to outline his plans for the new season.

"I want to add a Champions League run into the mix," Jürgen announced. "We've been in it for a few years now, but we've not made a lot of progress. So this is the year we're going to announce ourselves as one of the big guns in Europe."

Robert's mood instantly picked up. It was always inspiring to witness his manager's enthusiasm and vision. But now Jürgen was focusing on a competition that Robert was keen to excel in.

He remembered watching Champions League games on the TV with his dad, and spending hours discussing them afterwards.

After Jürgen had finished his team talk he sent the players out for their training session. Robert immediately headed over to new signing Marco Reus.

The pair had struggled to build an effective partnership in the Super Cup game and he didn't want a repeat of that in any Champions League matches.

"So how do you want the ball played into you?" Robert asked Marco.

"I tend to cut in from the left – on my right," Marco replied, showing the motion with his hands. The German winger was equally keen to work this all out sooner rather than later.

"Well, I can try and slip the passes through to you if you get in behind," Robert replied. "I'll hold back and if you look up you might be able to pull it back to me."

Marco nodded and the pair high-fived, before heading over to the pitch to polish their moves.

Hopefully, a new trophy depended on it.

When Robert had first seen Dortmund's Champions League group, he'd been glad that he'd worked as hard as he had with Marco in training. It included Dutch champions Ajax, Spanish champions Real Madrid and English champions Manchester City.

The Dortmund team had been a little spooked, but

Jürgen had been quick to remind them they were the German champions, and a force to be reckoned with.

He'd been right, and Dortmund had stunned the world as they'd eased their way to the top of that group.

Then, with the sense of vigour that only came from beating teams of that standard, they'd continued to climb the Champions League ladder.

They'd cruised past Shakhtar Donetsk of Ukraine and drawn 0-0 away from home against Malaga. It meant they only needed a home win against Malaga to go through to the semis.

With less than ten minutes to go, Malaga were leading 2-1. The away goals rule that had come to haunt many a side in this competition was about to bite Dortmund – they needed two goals in seven minutes if they were to go through.

Robert glanced at the clock and fought back a sense of panic. Wasn't this a virtually impossible task?

Nonetheless, Dortmund continued to push and suddenly, on 91 minutes, the ball was played into the penalty area. Marco fired it home and levelled the scores at 2-2. Could there be a glimmer of hope?

Robert could see Jürgen waving and shouting on the touchline. He understood how his manager was feeling – they were just too close to throw it away now.

"We can do this, lads!" Robert roared, firing up the players around him. "One more chance is all we need!"

He was right. A free kick was pumped into the area and Julian Schieber swung at the ball. It fell to the feet of big centre-back Felipe Santana, who tapped it across the line.

GOAL!

The Signal Iduna Park erupted. The Malaga players desperately appealed for offside, but their cries were waved away by the ref.

Borussia Dortmund had done the impossible and they were now through to the semi-finals. Robert looked up to the sky and gave his dad a little nod, to celebrate the fact that their Champions League dream was still alive.

"Well, we've already beaten them once," Mario Götze said half-heartedly. The rest of the Dortmund team looked at him, signs of nerves showing on most of their faces.

It was the day of the semi-finals and the mood in the Dortmund dressing room was sombre.

Real Madrid – including Sergio Ramos, Mesut Özil, Luka Modric and, of course, Cristiano Ronaldo – were waiting for them just outside this room.

Robert smiled at Mario. In some ways the midfielder was right. They *had* beaten Real Madrid in the group stages, but Robert knew that the team they were about to face was going to be very different. In this semi-final they were going to be twice as hungry and twice as dangerous.

The thought made Robert very grateful that this first leg was at home, and as he walked out onto the pitch he hoped that the Dortmund players were using the raucous noise from their fans to settle any nerves.

He told himself firmly that he just needed an early goal, one that would give the rest of the team some confidence.

A few minutes later an inch-perfect cross from Mario flew in his direction. It slipped through all the Real Madrid defenders, but not past Robert. He stretched out a leg and his toe connected with the ball, propelling it into the bottom corner.

GOAL!

Robert couldn't have asked for a better start.

That goal took Dortmund a step closer to the final, and it also took Robert a step closer to winning another, less official, competition he was constantly thinking about: Ronaldo v Lewandowski.

Robert had seen this game being billed in the press as a battle between the two strikers and he was desperate to prove he was worthy of being mentioned in the same breath as the legend.

Now he was on the way to doing that. He just had to keep it together.

The game got back underway and, as Robert hoped, the early lead gave his team-mates confidence. Dortmund were completely dominant, but they struggled to make their chances count and, minutes before the break, Cristiano struck.

Now it was Dortmund 1-1 Real Madrid, and Ronaldo 1-1 Lewandowksi.

"We need to start making those chances count," Jürgen said as he gathered them into the dressing room at half-time. "We've got the opportunity of a lifetime here."

The players knew what they had to do and they worked hard to make sure the second half started just as brightly as the first.

Then Marco smuggled the ball into the box and passed it to Robert, who spun and poked it under Diego López and into the Real Madrid goal, to make it 2-1.

Robert was thrilled to have scored a second goal, but he reigned in his celebrations, only jogging lightly towards the fans and punching the air. The match wasn't over yet and he needed to be composed, ready for his next opportunity.

It came less than five minutes later, when Marcel Schmelzer fired the ball across the box. Robert was there to receive it. He controlled the ball with his first touch, killing its speed. Then, as the defenders closed him down, he dragged the ball back and, with it slightly behind him, he swung at it.

GOAL!

This time Robert couldn't contain his celebrations. It was his first Champions League hat-trick, and he wasn't just keeping up with Ronaldo in their unspoken competition, he was blowing him out of the water.

"How did you do that, Robbie?" Mario shouted, as a pack of Dortmund players chased Robert to the corner flag. "That was genius!"

A short while later, Marco Reus was taken out in the Real Madrid penalty area. The referee instantly pointed to the spot and the whole Dortmund team knew that there was only one man for the job.

Robert stepped up, calm as always. He'd already decided simply to put his foot through it. The ball sailed past the keeper for the fourth time, rippling the back of the net.

The stadium erupted. Dortmund were doing exactly what Jürgen had said they would do – making a statement to the rest of Europe.

The rest of the game passed without further incident. A second leg was now all that stood between Dortmund and the final, and Robert's eyes were fixed on the next prize for his trophy cabinet.

Jakub and Łukasz, who'd both been subbed off late in the match, came sprinting over to him at full time.

"Are you running some kind of striker's masterclass?" Łukasz said as he clapped him on the back.

"Forget Cristiano Ronaldo! This is Robert Lewandowski's tournament!" Jakub announced to anyone that could hear him over the roaring of the fans.

14
THE FINAL FOE

May 2013, Wembley Stadium, London, England
Borussia Dortmund v Bayern Munich

Robert was experienced enough to know that football could be insanely dramatic, but even he couldn't believe the wicked twist the Champions League had in store.

After surviving their second leg against Real Madrid at the Bernabéu, Dortmund were through to the final –to meet Bayern Munich.

It was going to be the first ever all-German

Champions League final, and the anticipation was only heightened by rumours leading up to the game that Mario had agreed to join Bayern next season for around 40 million euros.

There were a lot of strong feelings surrounding the rumours and Robert had been worried that Mario's supposed departure would become a distraction on final day. But as it turned out, the midfielder was ruled out of the game with an injury, leaving the Dortmund team free to focus on the challenge ahead of them.

And it was a big one.

Dortmund had failed to beat Bayern in all three competitions back home this season, and Jürgen could sense the nervous energy in the dressing room before the match.

"We know what Bayern are about, and we know what we need to do to beat them," the manager said sternly. "So let's go out there and do it!"

Robert was the only player who didn't need to hear Jürgen's words of encouragement. It didn't matter who he had to beat to get this trophy – after his performance against Real Madrid, together with the fact that he'd won the Golden Boot for his 24 goals in the Bundesliga this season, he was up for it.

In the tunnel he eyed up the Bayern wingers who he deemed to be the biggest threat – Franck Ribéry and Arjen Robben. His instincts were correct and after a dull first half it was Robben who made the difference.

Robben had burst away down the left, weaving his way past a number of Dortmund defenders, managing to get the ball to Mario Mandžukic in the box. He tapped it home first time.

Bayern led.

Robert kept his composure, knowing the game was far from over, and sure enough 10 minutes later Bayern defender Dante put his foot into the chest of Marco Reus. It was instantly a penalty.

"Go on, İlkay!" Robert bellowed, pushing the number eight forward. "You're our first-choice penalty taker."

İlkay Gündoğan stepped up and comfortably tucked the ball home. Now it was 1-1, all to play for.

Both sides held firm and the game looked as if it was heading for extra time, when Arjen Robben made the difference once again. He burst in and managed to scuff the ball past keeper Weidenfeller. There was nothing Dortmund could do.

Bayern had won the most dramatic final in the most sensational fashion, and it took Robert a second to accept that the dream was over.

He collapsed to his knees.

"We did incredibly well to get this far," Jürgen reassured Robert calmly, once he'd finally managed to stumble in off the pitch.

Robert nodded mechanically, but it didn't make him feel any better.

Jürgen was the one who always reminded him that, whenever you reach the top, you should find a new top to reach. Knowing he'd just blown a huge opportunity to reach his 'next top' really hurt.

He looked back over his shoulder at the celebrations on the pitch and took a deep breath. His dream might be over, but it was only over until next season.

He'd be back. Next season he'd do whatever it took to be the one lifting that cup.

15

DORTMUND DOUBT

July 2013, Dortmund training ground,
Dortmund, Germany

The rumours floating around before the Champions League final were proved right. Mario had departed for Bayern Munich, and Robert couldn't stop thinking about his friend's move.

He recalled the conversation he'd had with him when the story had first come out.

"Mario, is it true? Are you going to Bayern?" he'd

asked, when they had a private moment. Robert didn't want to create an embarrassing situation for his friend.

"I don't want to think about it until the final deal is done," Mario had replied, looking at the floor. Robert had nodded, feeling sympathetic. As far as he was concerned, Mario was right to go to Bayern if it was the right place for him.

Robert had been questioning his own presence at Dortmund as well, ever since that Bayern final. They'd finished the season without a single trophy, which by their previous standards was a major disappointment.

He couldn't help but wonder if the team had peaked already, and if the 'new era' of German football was already over. All he knew for sure was that he didn't want the highlight of his career to be losing in a final to Bayern Munich.

And if Dortmund were a club who sold their best players to their biggest rivals, how were they ever going to improve? His personal goals might have been in sync with Dortmund's at one stage, but he just wasn't convinced that this was the case any more.

"I'm just a little worried, boss," Robert explained to

Jürgen before the new season began. "Mario's gone to Bayern, they've got Pep Guardiola in, and they won just about everything last year ... How are we going to get anywhere near them?"

"We've got some good players coming in," Jürgen replied casually. "There's Aubameyang, Mhikitaryan, Sokratis ... " He continued listing the names of a number of their summer signings, counting them out on his hand.

"I don't doubt those guys are good, but how long is it going to take them to adapt?" Robert asked. "By the time they're used to the Bundesliga, Bayern might have won it again already."

Jürgen nodded, finally appreciating the seriousness of Robert's complaints.

"The only thing I need you to do, Robert, is sign a new contract," he said finally. "Yours is up next summer and if you commit to your future here, then that will help us bring in some bigger players. Alright?"

Robert paused. He was flattered that his name in a team made such an impact, and signing that contract seemed to be the right choice for Dortmund. But what about him? He'd made himself a promise in his mum's living room, when he'd been younger, that he was going to be the best, whatever it took. It was that promise that had brought him here in the first place.

"I can't make that commitment, boss."

Jürgen glared at him but Robert forced himself to stay strong. He'd always been ruthless in the box and he knew he would have to be just as ruthless here, with the manager that had given him his big chance.

"There are things I want to do and I don't think I'll be able to do them at Dortmund. I think it's time I left – either now, so you can get some money, or for free next year when my contract expires."

Jürgen's glare melted into a sad little smile. Robert would be a huge loss, but in many ways the manager wasn't surprised to be losing him. He'd dealt with athletes his entire life and the best ones were the best for a reason – they pushed themselves relentlessly. It meant they were people who would always be prepared to move on if they had to.

"Ok, Rob. I'll talk to the board and see if we can sort out a move for you before the season starts."

Robert had expected to have left the club before the start of the season, but when the German Super Cup rolled around he found himself training for it alongside the rest of the lads.

He'd heard nothing from the board since his conversation with Jürgen and, despite the growing number of rumours in the press, he'd heard nothing from his agent either.

It meant that his mind was elsewhere during the match and he didn't manage to contribute a single goal to Dortmund's 4-2 victory over Bayern Munich.

It had been a poor performance, and he couldn't believe it when he saw Bayern's new manager, Pep Guardiola, walking over to him after the match.

"Robert, hello. I've been looking forward to meeting you," Pep said, reaching out his hand and grasping Robert's. Despite the defeat, Pep was buzzing with energy. "It was great to watch you out there – I do hope you'll consider us as an option for yourself one day."

Robert was caught off guard by Pep's words. *Us?* As in 'Bayern Munich'? He hadn't even considered

Dortmund's big rivals as an option, and he felt a little guilty at being so excited by it.

"It's great to meet you too," he replied. "You should definitely talk to the board. They – "

"Ah, we've already spoken with the board," Pep interrupted. "They say you're not for sale. So I'm just letting you know, we'd love to talk about the prospect of you joining us next summer."

Before Robert had an opportunity to reply, Pep was dragged off by a few members of his coaching staff, who were eager to review the match with him.

Robert stood, digesting what he'd just heard. If Bayern were interested, why hadn't the Dortmund board said anything to him? And why would they say he wasn't for sale?

He swiftly made his way off the pitch and found somewhere private to ring Cezary.

"So Bayern are trying to sign me?" he clarified.

"Yes, but Dortmund don't want to sell you," his agent replied, a little surprised to be having this conversation. "They've decided they'd rather lose you for free next year than sell you to Bayern now."

Robert sighed. He felt a little betrayed that no one had let him know, but he understood that Jürgen and the board were just looking after the club's best interests.

Cezary continued. "They might be doing it to appease the people who're still angry about the club selling Mario ... or they could be hoping you'll change your mind and sign a new contract."

Robert clutched the phone tightly as he thought it all through. Bayern were one of the biggest clubs in the world, and playing for them would open up amazing doors for him.

He'd desperately miss his friends, especially Jakub and Łukasz, but he knew they'd get to play together again in the national team. Nothing had changed since he'd had that meeting with Jürgen – he was too far up the ladder he'd spent his life climbing to stop now.

"Cezary, I want you to talk to Bayern and agree a deal for me to join them next summer," he said firmly.

And with that he ended the call.

16
A BAYERN BOY

July 2014, Bayern Munich training ground,
Munich, Germany

As Robert walked around Bayern Munich's training ground on his first day, he almost had to pinch himself. He was finally here, walking the halls of one of the best clubs in the world, on his way to the start-of-season team talk.

Continuing to play for Dortmund, while knowing he was Bayern-bound, had been tough, and his last season there had seemed to drag on and on. However in terms of goals it had still been exceptional – he'd won the Bundesliga Golden Boot again and had also become Dortmund's record goal scorer in European competitions.

But, as he'd predicted, Dortmund had finished well off the pace in the Bundesliga and had been dumped out of the Champions League.

It had given him strength in his conviction that he was right to be leaving, even though some of the fans and players had turned against him.

Keeping in touch with Mario had helped him deal with that. The midfielder had understood Robert's tricky situation better than anybody, and he helped keep Robert's spirits up.

One subject consistently kept up Robert's enthusiasm for the move.

"So what's he like? Pep?" Robert had asked Mario over the phone on more than one occasion. The only time he'd spoken to his future manager had been on the pitch after the Super Cup that day, and he was desperate to know more about the man who'd 'made' Messi.

"He's quite similar to Jürgen," Mario had mused. "He's always talking – and it's quite hard to work out what he means half the time."

Now, as he took his seat at today's team talk, Robert could see that Mario's description of the manager was pretty much spot-on.

"The league, the cup, the Champions League," Pep said. He spoke quickly and never stopped moving his hands. "Those are our targets. If we don't win all three, then we have failed. Do you understand? If we win all three but the fans go home bored, then we have also failed. You understand?"

Robert wasn't the only new arrival at the club, and he looked over to Sebastian Rode, Juan Bernat and Xabi Alonso. They all looked just as perplexed by their new manager, but just as fired up as well.

By the time Pep's talk was over, Robert was itching to get on the training pitch and it was there that he started to see the big difference between his old manager and his new one.

At Dortmund there had been an emphasis on getting the ball into the other team's half as soon as possible, whereas at Bayern it was all about holding on to the ball. As he'd already heard Pep say four times today, "If the other team don't have the ball, they can't score."

As a result, as Robert began to realise, everyone at Bayern was incredibly good at passing. He watched Mario and Phillip Lahm ping passes to each other across the training pitch, each one landing at the other's feet with uncanny precision.

Arjen Robben caught him watching and laughed. "It's how Pep wants it," he explained. "We do a lot of slow passes round the back and then suddenly we go into quick, fast-paced passing. The opposition can't keep up with it. He calls it tiki-taka … "

"Oh, what Barcelona do," Robert said with a nod. If it was good enough for Barcelona, it was certainly good enough for him, and he got stuck right in with Arjen, casting aside the strange feeling that came with practising alongside someone he'd previously always considered a threat.

The session went by in a flash and Robert was pleasantly surprised to find that it all seemed pretty easy. The last time he'd moved clubs was four years ago, to Dortmund, and he still remembered how hard he had found the change.

As he headed to the showers, it suddenly struck him that he must already be playing at Bayern's level – the level that could win the Champions League and everything else in between.

It was, as Jürgen had once explained to him – Dortmund *made* superstars.

As if confirming this realisation, a few days later he was given the number nine shirt. Its previous owner, Mario Mandžukić, had just moved to Atlético Madrid. It was an immediate show of faith and Robert couldn't thank Pep enough for making him his main man.

"Thank me with goals," the Spaniard had said, with a wink.

17
FIVE IN NINE

September 2015, Allianz Arena, Munich, Germany
Bayern Munich v Wolfsburg

Robert had racked up 20 goals in his first season at Bayern. It had helped the club seal a Bundesliga title and confirmed once and for all to Robert that the move had been the right decision.

The one disappointment had been getting knocked out of the Champions League by Pep's old side, Barcelona. Robert was gutted that he'd have to wait yet another year to try again in the competition, but he had no one to blame but himself. For whatever reason – whether it was playing at the Nou Camp or being star-struck by the legends on Barcelona's side – he'd had few flashes at goal and he'd wasted them all.

The only upside of the match had been having the chance to watch Messi. There had been about 10 world-class players on the pitch, but the little Argentinian had still been miles above everyone else.

It was exactly what Robert aspired to be, and he used it as motivation as he trained hard for his second season with Bayern.

Some of his team-mates found it bizarre that, at this stage in his career, he was still the first one out on the pitch and the last one off it.

"What are you trying to prove, man? You're Robert Lewandowski!"

Robert laughed at himself with them, but really he didn't get it – there was always something else to be achieved, and he wanted to make the most of what came his way.

That was the attitude he brought to the next game

against Wolfsburg. He was starting on the bench, nursing a slight injury, and he was forced to watch Bayern struggle to make an impact.

Wolfsburg took an early lead and at half-time an impatient Pep turned to Robert.

"Get on there," Pep said, clapping him on the back. "Show them how it's done!"

Five minutes after coming on, Robert had his first goal. Arturo Vidal burst into the box and, after a slight scramble, the ball fell to Robert's feet. He quickly poked it into the back of the net.

"You guys can't do anything without me, can you?" he joked to Thomas Müller from behind his hand.

Wolfsburg kicked the game back off, but almost instantly gave the ball away. The ball bounced its way through their defence and Robert picked it up on the edge of the box. He spun round and fired off a shot. It whipped off the grass and went past the keeper.

He'd scored two goals in two minutes!

"Imagine how many you'd have by now if you'd started the game!" Arturo laughed, as the team gathered round Robert, completely in awe of him.

A few minutes later, Bayern broke again. Thomas had burst forward and found Mario, who in turn slipped the ball across for Robert. His first shot cannoned off the post, but it came straight back to him. He was able to juggle it over a defender and then around the keeper, to stab it into the net.

Now he'd secured a hat-trick in the space of about four minutes.

"That's got to be some kind of record!" someone shouted in Robert's direction, but the comment fell on deaf ears. There was an atmosphere in the stadium that suggested something special was happening, and Robert wanted to see how far he could take it.

In no time Douglas Costa had burst away down the left-hand side and was whipping in a cross. Robert came sprinting on to it and crashed the ball into the back of the net. Four.

"I was thinking you hadn't scored for a while, Rob!" Mario joked breathlessly. Like everyone else in the stadium, he was stunned by his team-mate.

A couple more minutes passed, and once more Bayern broke. Mario got into some space down the right-hand side and lifted the ball towards Robert. It was still moving quickly when Robert threw himself into the air and fired a volley at goal. It flew past the keeper, shaking the net with the power of his strike.

The team ran over to celebrate with him for the fifth time, but no one spoke a word. They had never seen anything like it and they were utterly speechless.

Pep was standing on the touchline, eyes wide, mouth open, with his hands held to his face. Next to him, one of the coaches was mouthing that Robert had scored five goals in nine minutes.

After Bayern's 5-1 victory was confirmed and after watching the replay after the game, even Robert couldn't believe what he'd managed to do.

"It's iconic," Pep said simply, over Robert's shoulder.

It wasn't long before the Guinness Book of World Records were in touch to arrange a press conference, where Robert would receive not one, but *four* certificates for the four records he'd broken:

- ✪ The highest number of goals scored by a substitute in the Bundesliga.
- ✪ The fastest Bundesliga hat-trick.

✪ The fastest four goals in a Bundesliga match.

✪ The fastest five goals in a Bundesliga match.

When Robert heard the news, he simply smiled. He'd like to see Messi do that.

18
PRIDE AND PENS

June 2016, Stade Vélodrome, Marseille, France
Poland v Portugal

Once again, Robert found himself lining up for a game that was being billed as 'Lewandowski v Ronaldo', but this time it was an even bigger affair. This time, the pair were representing their countries, head to head.

When Robert had first arrived in France for the Euros he'd been eager to get started. As well as being named as Poland's captain, he was playing the best football of his life back in Germany and he'd felt confident he was in the best position possible to lead the team beyond the group stages this year.

However, it had been a bumpy start and Robert had actually struggled in the group games, feeling the effects of a long season where Bayern had stormed to a league and a cup double.

But with the help of his strike partner, Arkadiusz Milik, Poland had scrambled their way into the quarter finals.

Once a nation that barely qualified for international tournaments, Poland were now here, taking on Portugal in the last eight.

Robert could see Cristiano out of the corner of his eye as he took his place on the pitch, but he kept his mind focused.

He was part of a Poland squad that had gone further in the Euros than any before it – exactly what he'd wanted since his very first appearance for his country – and he was ready to give everything he had in this tournament.

And, only two minutes in, Robert struck. The ball

was pulled back to him from the left-hand side and with his first touch he slammed it into the goal.

Overjoyed, he ran towards the corner flag, even though Jakub was hanging off his neck. The noise was unlike anything he'd heard before – the thousands of Polish fans who'd made the trip to France were starting to believe.

Poland kept the lead for about half an hour, until the young midfielder Renato Sanches whipped the ball into the bottom corner to bring Portugal level.

Robert looked up to the sky for inspiration. He knew his dad was watching, and he wasn't going to give up that easily.

Poland continued to fight against the more experienced Portuguese side for the full 90 minutes – and then into extra time. With the scores still level, they were now to be exposed to the lottery of a penalty shootout.

Robert glanced at the Portugal side and saw Ronaldo inspiring his players, and he attempted to do the same.

"We did it, lads!" he roared. "We held one of the favourites to win this competition to a draw. Penalties can go either way – we've got absolutely nothing to lose here!"

He then turned and watched as Cristiano put his penalty away.

Robert put his penalty away next, trying to lead by example, and, as he walked back to take his place amongst his team, he made eye contact with Cristiano.

There was now nothing more either of them could do and Robert was just quietly happy he'd managed to score in open play, when his rival had not.

Arm-in-arm with his team-mates, Robert watched as each player stood up to the mark.

Devastatingly, it was Jakub who missed his penalty. It was the slimmest of margins, but Portugal had won – and Poland were out.

Robert's heart sank, but this time he put his own emotions aside. After all their years of friendship, after everything Jakub had done for him at Dortmund, all he wanted to do was console his friend, who he knew would be crushed by his penalty miss.

"It doesn't matter, OK? We've done insanely well,"

Robert comforted Jakub after following him off the pitch and into the dressing room.

It was the truth. Even getting this far had heralded a new era of Polish football, and their fans were still letting them know it, their applause for today's valiant effort audible through the walls.

"And what's more, we'll be back in no time to do even better," Robert continued.

Jakub nodded sadly, and took a deep sniff before forcing a little smile.

"Well done *you*, though. I heard them say your goal was the second-fastest in Euros history. The whole world will be chanting your name!"

Robert paused, struck by his friend's words. Despite today's defeat, he had the same kind of feeling he usually got when he'd won something.

"That's why my dad named me Robert," he said quietly. "He thought it was a name that would be easy to say all around the world, for when I became a footballer."

Jakub put his arm around him. "Seriously, well done then, mate. You certainly haven't wasted it."

19

FOREVER RONALDO'S RIVAL

April 2017, Allianz Arena, Munich, Germany
Bayern Munich v Real Madrid

It had been a long time since Robert had watched a game from the stands and he was enjoying being in the thick of the electrifying atmosphere that football fans create. It took him right back to watching matches with his family when he was younger, and helped make up for the disappointment of being ruled out of this particular game with a shoulder injury.

Not only was Bayern's opponent Real Madrid, a team he always relished the chance to beat, but it was a Champions League quarter final. This competition was still something he needed to win, and he had a good feeling about their chances this year, under new manager Carlo Ancelotti.

At first he hadn't been sure there could be any kind of silver lining when he'd heard the news that Pep was leaving Bayern for Man City.

But Carlo's arrival had brought some positives. He was a manager who'd won the Champions League more than once, and Robert could already see some improvements on the pitch.

The game had got off to a cracking start for Bayern Munich. A cross from Thiago was met by a bullet header from Arturo Vidal that hit the back of the net.

Robert rose from his seat with the rest of the Bayern fans to celebrate the goal. Then he sat back down with a grin, amused by the thought that his team-mates might have actually listened to the jokey warning he'd put on their group chat earlier that day:

> I might be back for the second leg, so make sure there's still a game for me to rescue.

His enjoyment, however, quickly turned to frustration as he watched Bayern miss chance after chance.

"You've *got* to be scoring that," he muttered to himself, slapping his thigh in anger.

Bayern couldn't make their dominance count and at half-time they only led 1-0. A couple of minutes into the second half Cristiano Ronaldo made them pay, equalising for Real. With Poland's exit from the Euros last year still fresh in his mind, Robert couldn't hide his displeasure.

From that point on, it was a miracle that Real only ran out 2-1 winners. Robert could only close his eyes and pray that he'd be back for the second leg. He couldn't face going home from this competition empty-handed one more time.

He did a couple of shoulder rolls out on the Bernabéu

pitch and took a deep breath. Robert's prayers had been answered and he'd recovered enough to play in the return leg in Madrid.

The first half had been deeply frustrating and, although Bayern had been dominant, they were still level with Real Madrid at 0-0.

The chance to change that came early in the second half, when Arjen Robben was taken out in the box. The ref instantly pointed to the spot and Robert stepped up. With his usual precision, he hammered the ball into the back of the net.

Bayern's lead, however, was only temporary and Ronaldo struck an equaliser barely 15 minutes later.

Robert quickly realised that he would have to come up with something better than a penalty, but he could sense the beginnings of despair amongst his team-mates.

"One more goal and we take this to extra time, lads!" he shouted, trying to keep them focused.

It worked, and Bayern got the ball back into the box, where a mix-up in the Real Madrid back four led to Ramos poking the ball past his own keeper.

Bayern Munich were very much back in the tie.

The game went into extra time, but once again Bayern were bettered in the Champions League. Cristiano struck twice in five minutes, before Marco Asensio sealed the win for Real Madrid.

It took everything Robert had not to collapse to his knees at full-time. He couldn't believe that *yet again* he'd been beaten in this tournament.

As he turned, he noticed a shadow darken the grass in front of him. He looked up to see who'd come over.

"You just won't let me win anything, will you?" Robert said, with a slight smile.

"Nope," Cristiano smiled back. "But I can remember some games you didn't let me win, either."

There weren't many people on this planet who could be considered a match for Cristiano Ronaldo and, as Robert shook the hand of one of the greatest footballers of all time, he felt a sense of calm at today's result.

He would return to Germany – and to what looked to be his best season yet – and he would come back next year, better than ever before.

That was his job – and it was without doubt the best job in the world.

20
200 AND COUNTING

September 2019, Allianz Arena, Munich, Germany
Red Star Belgrade v Bayern Munich

Serbian side Red Star Belgrade had been weathering
the Bayern Munich storm, but now cracks were starting
to show in their defence.

These were the kind of cracks a player like Robert
would always exploit and, after Kingsley Coman had
headed home a goal, Robert scrambled one into the
net.

Even after all these years, scoring sent a shiver of excitement through him.

Thomas Müller also managed to get a goal before the game was done and the final whistle saw Bayern hammering Red Star Belgrade 3-0.

As the celebrations started, Robert noticed that none of the Bayern coaching staff had run on to the pitch and were instead whispering excitedly in a little huddle.

It piqued his interest, but he was soon distracted by the celebrations on the pitch.

"Good stuff out there today, Serge," he said, as he crossed paths with the winger who'd been subbed on late in the match.

"Thanks, Rob," Serge stuttered, wide-eyed.

Robert recognised his expression as being like the one he'd probably had when he'd been complimented by Raúl, all those years ago. He smiled at the thought that the young winger could still be star-struck by his presence, after more than a year of their playing together.

The Bayern celebrations started to move to the changing rooms and Robert was just about to follow them when he noticed the coaching staff again. They were still standing on the touchline, but were now staring directly at him.

He felt compelled to go over.

"Robert, that was your 200th goal for Bayern Munich," one of the coaches blurted out. "We kept track."

Robert was stunned. He looked around at the other coaches' faces, as if to confirm that the absurdly large number was true. Every one of them was nodding and smiling.

He really had scored 200 goals, and that was just in his time with Bayern. He stood for a moment trying to work out what the number would be if they took into account all the clubs he'd played for. MKS Varsovia Warsaw, Delta Warsaw, Legia Warsaw, Znicz Pruszków, Lech Poznań and Borussia Dortmund had all come before Bayern.

"That's incredible, guys. But I couldn't have done it without you," he said to the gaggle of coaches, before excusing himself and heading down the tunnel.

Reflecting on his long, winding journey to get to this

point had given Robert an immense sense of pride in his achievements.

He was proud that he hadn't let rejection, and the fact that he'd practically had to start his career again at the age of seventeen, stop him from achieving his dreams. In fact, he'd used that setback to become all the more determined to claw his way up the ladder and become the player he was today.

A player who'd broken an abundance of records while helping his teams to greatness, a player who'd scored the opening goal of a Euros competition in his home country, a player who could be considered a match for Cristiano Ronaldo …

There was no doubt he'd honoured the promise he'd made to himself all those years ago – to do whatever it took to get to the top. He'd put in countless hours of hard work, made tough decisions and, at times, displayed pure grit.

That was what his dad would have been most proud of. Not the astonishing number of goals Robert had scored, so much as the strength he'd shown along the way in getting them.

The thought made him happy but, as ever, Robert wasn't content. Perhaps because his parents had both been athletes, and because being competitive was in his DNA, he was still just as ambitious now as he had been when he'd been a football-mad little boy playing-up in PE.

He continued walking down the tunnel, thinking about what he could achieve next.

Another Euros was on the horizon and the training sessions for the qualifiers had looked promising. Poland's new coach, Jerzy Brzęczek, was Jakub's uncle and the team felt more like a family than ever before.

And there was that one trophy he'd been chasing for years that still eluded him – the Champions League. It felt right that this milestone 200th goal should be in that very competition. With this win they were the early Group B leaders and his dream of being a champion of Europe was back within reach.

Robert finally reached the dressing room and opened the door to find his team-mates in high spirits, messing about together. It was an atmosphere he treasured and he stood there in the doorway, taking it all in.

He really did love this team, but he felt no shame in

knowing that he would leave them one day, if that's what it took to win what he wanted to win.

He'd been doing incredible things in the Bundesliga for years and the challenge of any one of the 'Big Five' leagues around Europe was one he welcomed.

He was, after all, 'Robert Lewandowski', arguably the best out-and-out striker in the world.

And he was showing no signs of slowing down.

21
AT LAST

August 2020, Estadio da Luz, Lisbon, Portugal
Champions League Final, Bayern Munich v PSG

"This is the only trophy you're missing, right?" Thomas Müller asked, clapping Robert on the back.

"Only because of you guys!" Robert chuckled.

There was a time when Robert wouldn't have joked about Dortmund's loss to Bayern in the 2013 final. But today, despite the pressure of the occasion, he felt relaxed.

But Thomas was right. The Champions League was the one trophy Robert hadn't won. Today, he had the chance to complete his collection.

The 2020 Champions League knockout stages had been unprecedented. The COVID pandemic had forced UEFA to hold the matches behind closed doors in Lisbon – this had meant that fans hadn't been allowed into the stadium.

"It's just a shame our fans can't be here," Robert said, glancing around the empty stadium.

"I think it will help us, though," Thomas answered.

Robert understood what Thomas meant. The Bayern fans could be demanding and unforgiving. If the game turned against the players, the fans might turn on them too. An empty stadium removed this pressure.

And there was already enough pressure to deal with. Bayern's opponents, PSG, were a quality side. Their team included the likes of Neymar, Mbappé and Di María. But Bayern had Robert – the best player in the world, right now.

Despite the heat and the tension, the first half was end-to-end. Robert fizzed a strike which deflected off the post, inches from opening the scoring. Then, he had a close-range header palmed away by the PSG keeper.

There were chances for PSG too, as Mbappé and Di María both squandered opportunities. At half-time the score remained 0-0. It was still all to play for.

Just 15 minutes into the second half, Bayern finally broke the deadlock, when Joshua Kimmich floated a dangerous cross into the box from the right wing. It flew over Robert's head, but fell perfectly for Kingsley Coman behind him.

Coman's header was perfect. Bayern had the lead.

Then, they went in search of a second goal to secure the win. Robert was denied multiple times by last-ditch blocks. But in the end, there were no more goals.

The game ended 1-0 – and Bayern were European Champions. Robert was a European Champion.

On the full-time whistle, he sank to his knees, overcome by emotion. The years of semi-final defeats, the defeat in the 2013 final, the one trophy that had been missing from his collection. He'd finally won it.

He could retire happy. His career could end tonight and he'd be content. But he still had more to do.

22
SEALED

May 2023, RCDE Stadium, Barcelona, Spain
Espanyol v Barcelona

Three years is a long time in football. Three years ago, Robert had sunk to his knees in Lisbon, as Bayern had clinched the Champions League.

Both the UEFA Super Cup and the Club World Cup had followed swiftly afterwards.

Hansi Flick, the manager who'd guided Bayern to victory, had left the club to take the job as Germany coach – and he'd been replaced by Julian Nagelsmann.

This turmoil hadn't impacted on Robert's form. He'd finished the 2020-21 season with 41 goals in the Bundesliga, smashing Gerd Müller's record that had stood for nearly 50 years. The following year, he'd scored 50 goals in all competitions.

No matter who was in charge, Robert was always going to score – and Bayern were always going to win the Bundesliga. But, once again, the Champions League seemed off limits to them. Two years in a row, they'd been dumped out in the quarter-finals, despite Robert's prolific goalscoring.

He needed a change. He found himself feeling the same thing that he'd felt at Dortmund all those years ago. He wanted a new challenge.

Due to his age, Bayern reluctantly let him depart, and for a relatively small fee of 50 million. There were a number of interested parties, but the one that captivated him was Barcelona.

They'd just lost Lionel Messi to PSG, and they needed a new superstar – someone to propel them back to the top.

Robert was the man for the job.

Any concerns that he would struggle in a new league had quickly been put to bed. He'd scored a brace in his second game for the club, and then a hat-trick in the Champions League. He'd taken his usual spot at the top of the goalscoring charts.

Despite this, Barcelona had been eliminated from the Champions League at the group stage. Robert would have to wait another year for more European success.

In La Liga, it was a different story. Since Robert's arrival, Barca had dominated the league – and in February they'd also beaten Real Madrid, to win the Spanish Super Cup.

Tonight, they had the opportunity to seal the La Liga title. All they needed to do was beat their local rivals, Espanyol.

The Barca starting line-up for the game was now a familiar one. The team included plenty of experience, with Robert in attack, Sergio Busquets anchoring the midfield, and ter-Stegen in goal.

These veterans were joined by quality youth players including Gavi, Pedri and Alejandro Balde.

Barca had become the possession-based pass masters

of Europe – a very different prospect to what Robert was used to in Bayern's high-intensity pressing system.

But Robert was the same lethal finisher he'd always been. No matter where he went, or who he played under, he never had difficulty finding the back of the net.

"A win is all we need today," Xavi, the Barca manager, had told the players before the game. "I don't care if it's a scrappy 1-0, or a comfortable 5-0. We've played the good football, now we just need to make sure we get the three points. Do that, and when you come back in here at full-time, you'll do so as champions."

Many of the Barca players were chasing their first league title. Robert was chasing his 12th, but he still felt the same hunger he always had.

Just ten minutes in, this combination of youth and experience led to Barca's first goal. Balde got away down the left wing and whipped a cross into the box.

As ever, Robert was in the right place at the right time. The ball fell perfectly to his feet and he poked it home to give Barcelona the lead. 1-0.

One quickly became two and, before half-time, two became three, when Robert smashed in his second goal from close range.

The win was sealed and so was the La Liga title.

Robert had another trophy under his belt. He'd proved that he could do it in multiple leagues – and in different countries.

He'd proved that he was one of the best players in the world.

He was now 34 years old, but he was still getting better. There were more records to break and more trophies to win. Robert was just as determined as he'd ever been.

Despite everything he'd won in his career, he still wasn't totally satisfied. He still had more to give, and he wasn't finished yet.

HOW MANY
HAVE YOU READ?

MESSI · KANE · RONALDO · HAALAND · SALAH

PULISIC · LEWANDOWSKI · RASHFORD · MBAPPÉ · SON

KANTÉ · VAN DIJK · NEYMAR